SCHOLASTIC

Reading & Writing
Graphic Organizers & Mini-Lessons

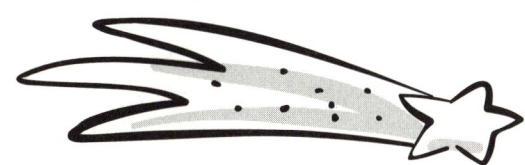

by Susan Van Zile

NEW YORK • TORONTO • LONDON • AUCKLAND • SYDNEY
MEXICO CITY • NEW DELHI • HONG KONG • BUENOS AIRES

Teaching Resources

Acknowledgments

To the Light of the World, with gratitude and thanksgiving for your gifts.
To Elaine Bergstresser, for her technical support, creative style, enthusiasm, and laughter.
To Tammy Novick, for her friendship and for providing many of the student examples in the text.
To my students, for their inspiration, joy, gifts, talents, and willingness to share.
Thank you for giving me hope for the future.
To my beloved family, for their encouragement and support.
To Virginia Dooley, Terry Cooper, and Scholastic, for educating and nurturing children.

Scholastic Inc. grants teachers permission to photocopy the reproducible pages from this book for classroom use. No other part of this publication may be reproduced in whole or in part, or stored in a retrieval system, or transmitted in any form or by any means, electronic, mechanical, photocopying, recording, or otherwise, without written permission of the publisher. For information regarding permission, write to Scholastic Inc., 557 Broadway, New York, NY 10012.

Cover design by Maria Lilja
Interior design by Jeffrey Dorman
Illustrations by Dave Clegg

ISBN 0-439-54897-7
Copyright © 2006 by Susan Van Zile
All rights reserved.
Printed in the USA.

2 3 4 5 6 7 8 9 10   40   12 11 10 09 08 07 06

Contents

Introduction 5

Reading

    KWL Chart 8

    Active Reading 10

    Powerful Predictions 12

    Keeping Track of Events 14

    Questions for Discussion 16

    Character Portrait 18

    Pleasing Plot 20

    Super Sequence 22

    Main Event Bridge 24

    Cause and Effect 26

Writing

    Blueprint for a Paragraph 28

    Satisfying Senses 30

    Nifty Narrative 32

    Perfectly Persuasive 34

    Excellent Essay 36

    Spectacular Story 38

    Sensational Summary 40

    Compare-Contrast Matrix 42

    Neat Notes for Research 44

    Simply Sources 46

Introduction

Remember the day you enthusiastically bounced into language arts class and exclaimed, "Now class, today we are going to write a story about the day the aliens invaded Wal-Mart!" You expected to see gleeful, smiling faces and hear shouts of joy; instead, 25 blank, staring, open-mouthed faces met your gaze. Not one to be easily discouraged, you took a deep breath and cheerfully responded, "Okay, I see you are not quite awake yet, so read the fabulous Ray Bradbury story that begins on page 35 of your anthology. It's one of my ultimate favorites!" Audible moans and groans echo in the room, frowns appear, and books slam onto desks.

Now, graphic organizers may not totally eradicate the blank stares or the complaints, but they will definitely improve the dismal picture. Even when a writing topic or a story inspires students, often they are discouraged because they do not know how to begin writing a story or how to tackle a text. Fortunately, graphic organizers can enhance both the reading and writing process, and, if used correctly, they can motivate students, too.

What Is a Graphic Organizer?

A graphic organizer is a visual and graphic representation of relationships among ideas and concepts. This instructional tool comes in a variety of formats—from loose webs to structured grids—that help students process information they've gathered and organize their ideas (Bromley et al., 1995).

For example, a series-of-events chain, such as "Super Sequence" (page 22) is used to show processes, sequences, causes and effects, or chronology. On the other hand, a matrix, such as "Compare-Contrast Matrix" (page 42), shows brainstorming, examples, attributes, and definitions. Other types of organizers include charts, webs, trees, and maps. Because graphic organizers are versatile, flexible, and visual, and because they use succinct language, they appeal to a variety of learners and help teachers differentiate instruction in inclusive classrooms.

Why Use Graphic Organizers?

Graphic organizers make teaching and learning more rewarding. Visually appealing and accessible to both struggling and advanced students, graphic organizers help students to:

- connect prior knowledge to new information (Guastello, 2000);
- integrate language and thinking in an organized format (Bromley et al., 1995);
- increase comprehension and retention of text (Boyle & Weishaar, 1997; Chang, K. et al, 2002; Moore & Readence, 1984);

- organize writing (Ellis, 1994);
- engage in mid- to high levels of thinking along Bloom's Taxonomy (application, analysis, evaluation, and synthesis) (Dodge, 2005).

How Are the Organizers Arranged in This Book?

The 20 graphic organizers in this book are designed to enhance reading and writing instruction. Many of the reading and writing organizers are interchangeable and can be used for various purposes.

The reading organizers aid students with before-, during-, and after-reading strategies. In addition, they encourage interaction with the text to increase comprehension. The writing organizers primarily address three types of writing: narrative, informational, and persuasive. They also help students organize single- and multiple-paragraph compositions.

Using the Lessons and Graphic Organizers in This Book

The organizers can be used flexibly for a variety of learning situations for students in grades 4–6: whole class, small groups, and individual students. Use them as motivational graphic aids to teach and practice skills and concepts, or use them as resources to support students in reading, writing, and researching.

Each lesson includes a skills focus, a statement of purpose, teaching suggestions, student samples, and a reproducible graphic organizer.

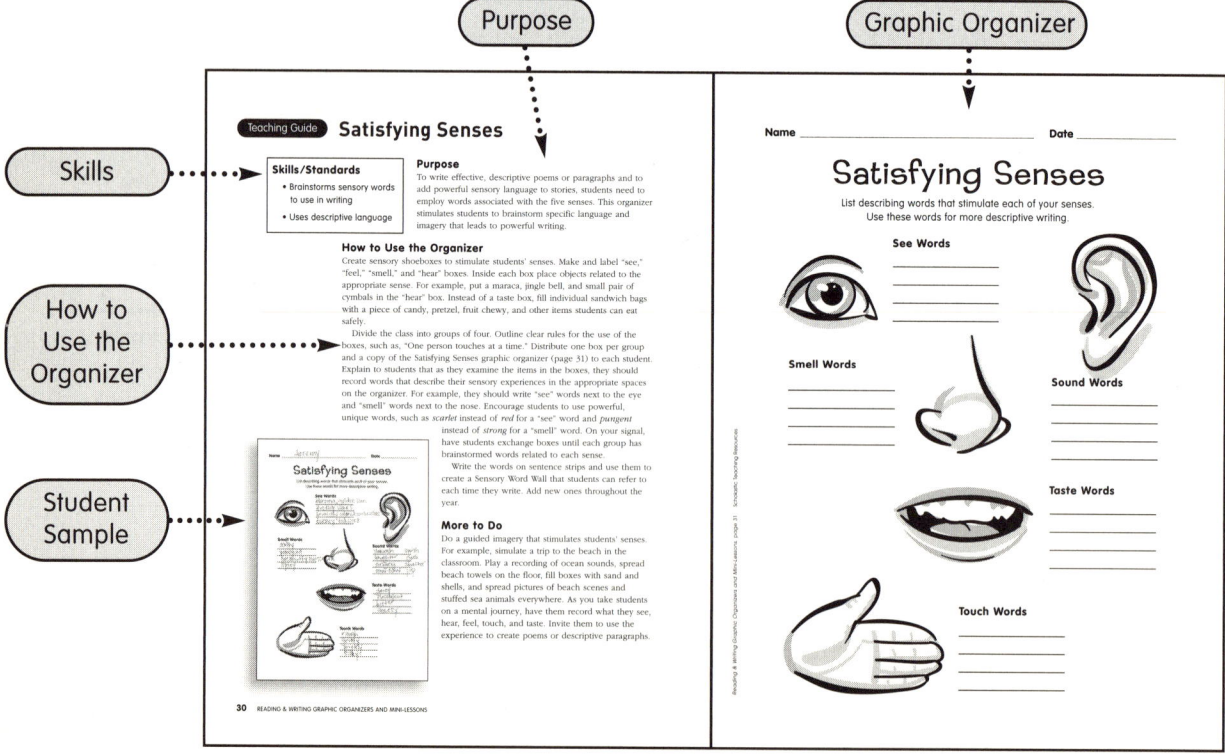

> One factor influencing the effectiveness of graphic organizers is the instructional context in which they are used. Studies suggest that to maximize the impact of graphic organizers on student learning, teachers need to state the purpose for using the organizer, model how to use it, and provide students with multiple opportunities for guided and independent practice and feedback.
>
> (National Center on Accessing the General Curriculum, 2002)

You can implement the organizers in any of the following ways:

- Draw the organizer on the board or on chart paper.
- Use the organizer as a template for an overhead transparency.
- Reproduce multiple copies of the organizer to pass out to students during class work.
- Have copies of the organizer available for students to use while reading and working independently.

For whole-class instruction, use the lessons and the graphic organizers to model how to organize information visually. Invite students to offer ideas and suggest where this information would go in the organizer; this helps build background for their own independent or small-group work.

For small-group instruction, use the lessons and graphic organizers to provide students with the opportunity to work and learn cooperatively. When students are familiar with the format and purpose of an organizer, you can adapt it for use as a game or group activity. As students build background and brainstorm together, their learning is enriched by one another's experiences.

For independent learning, use the graphic organizers to keep students engaged and focused on learning objectives. Once you've demonstrated how to complete the organizer, provide students with copies of the reproducible so they may complete their own during independent work time.

Use the lessons and graphic organizers in this book to help make reading and writing an exciting and successful part of your students' learning experience.

Teaching Guide: K-W-L Chart

Skills/Standards

- Previews text to activate prior knowledge
- Establishes a purpose for reading
- Reflects on what has been learned after reading

Purpose

Proficient readers scan the text before reading to activate prior knowledge. They also form questions that help set a purpose for reading, and they read to answer these questions. KWL is a strategy used to develop and enhance these skills. This organizer is particularly effective with expository text.

How to Use the Organizer

Choose an expository text to read with the class. Preview the selection, examining the title, headings, subheadings, visual aids, bold words, and chapter questions. Explain to students the importance of activating prior knowledge, setting a purpose for reading, and reading to achieve the purpose.

Distribute copies of the KWL organizer (page 9) to students and display a transparency copy on the overhead projector. Ask students: *What do you know about the topic?* Write their responses on the transparency while students record the information under the "What I Know" column on the organizer.

Next, have students formulate questions about what they want to know or discover about the topic. Write these on the transparency and ask students to list them under the "What I Want to Learn" column. Encourage students to add more questions as they read the selection.

During reading, as students find answers to their questions, have them record the information under the "What I Learned" column. When students have finished reading, review the questions they posed and discuss the answers they did and did not find.

More to Do

Use the KWL organizer as the foundation for a research project. Assign a topic or have students select one. After students activate their prior knowledge and form questions about the topic, take them to the media center to search for answers to their questions.

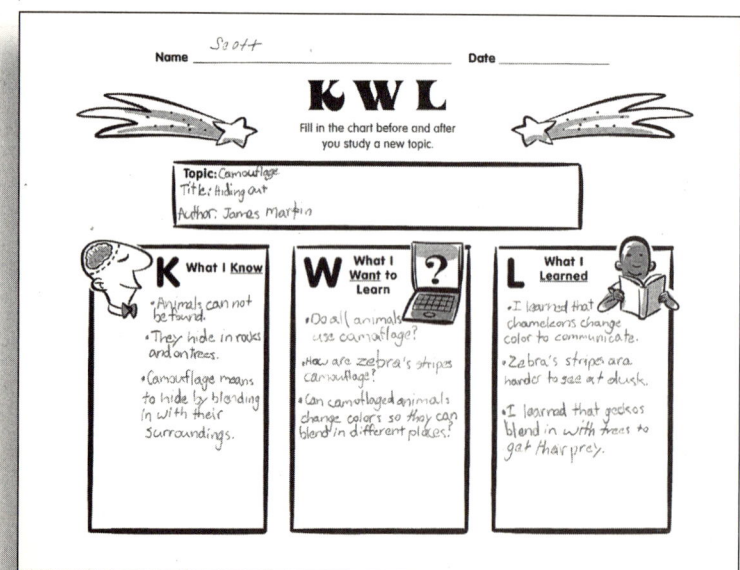

Name _____

Date _____

KWL

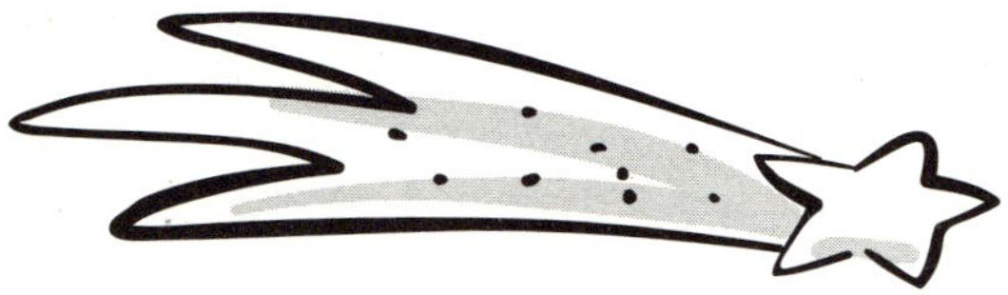

Fill in the chart before and after you study a new topic.

Topic: _____

K What I Know	**W** What I Want to Learn	**L** What I Learned

Reading & Writing Graphic Organizers & Mini-Lessons, page 9 — Scholastic Teaching Resources

Teaching Guide: Active Reading

Skills/Standards

- Asks questions about, makes connections, and responds to text
- Makes predictions about what is found in the text
- Uses mental images to aid in comprehension of text

Purpose

Proficient readers actively interact with text. They comprehend what they read because they ask questions, predict, visualize, connect, and respond to the text. Using this organizer will engage students in active reading.

How to Use the Organizer

Explain the active reading strategy (see above) to students and inform them that using this strategy will help them become better readers. Distribute copies of the Active Reading graphic organizer (page 11) and display a transparency copy on the overhead projector.

Model how to use the strategy by thinking aloud and verbalizing your thoughts as you read a story or portion of a text to the class. On the transparency, write down some of your questions, predictions, mental images (draw these), personal connections to the characters or events, and your feelings about or responses to the text.

Provide guided practice for students. Read a story with them and stop every once in a while to allow students to ask questions, make predictions, and share visualizations, connections, and responses. After students offer their responses, give them time to record their information in the appropriate section of the graphic organizer.

Give students frequent opportunities to practice and independently apply the active reading strategy to a variety of texts.

More to Do

Create active reading bookmarks. As students read a story or a chapter in a novel, have them record their responses on the bookmark.

For younger students or slower readers, focus on one aspect of the strategy at a time. For example, work on asking questions in one lesson and visualizing in another.

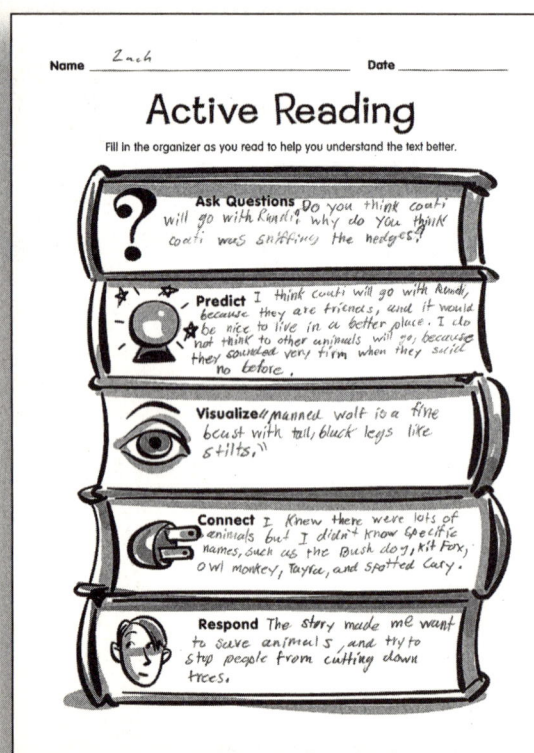

Name _____ Date _____

Active Reading

Fill in the organizer as you read to help you understand the text better.

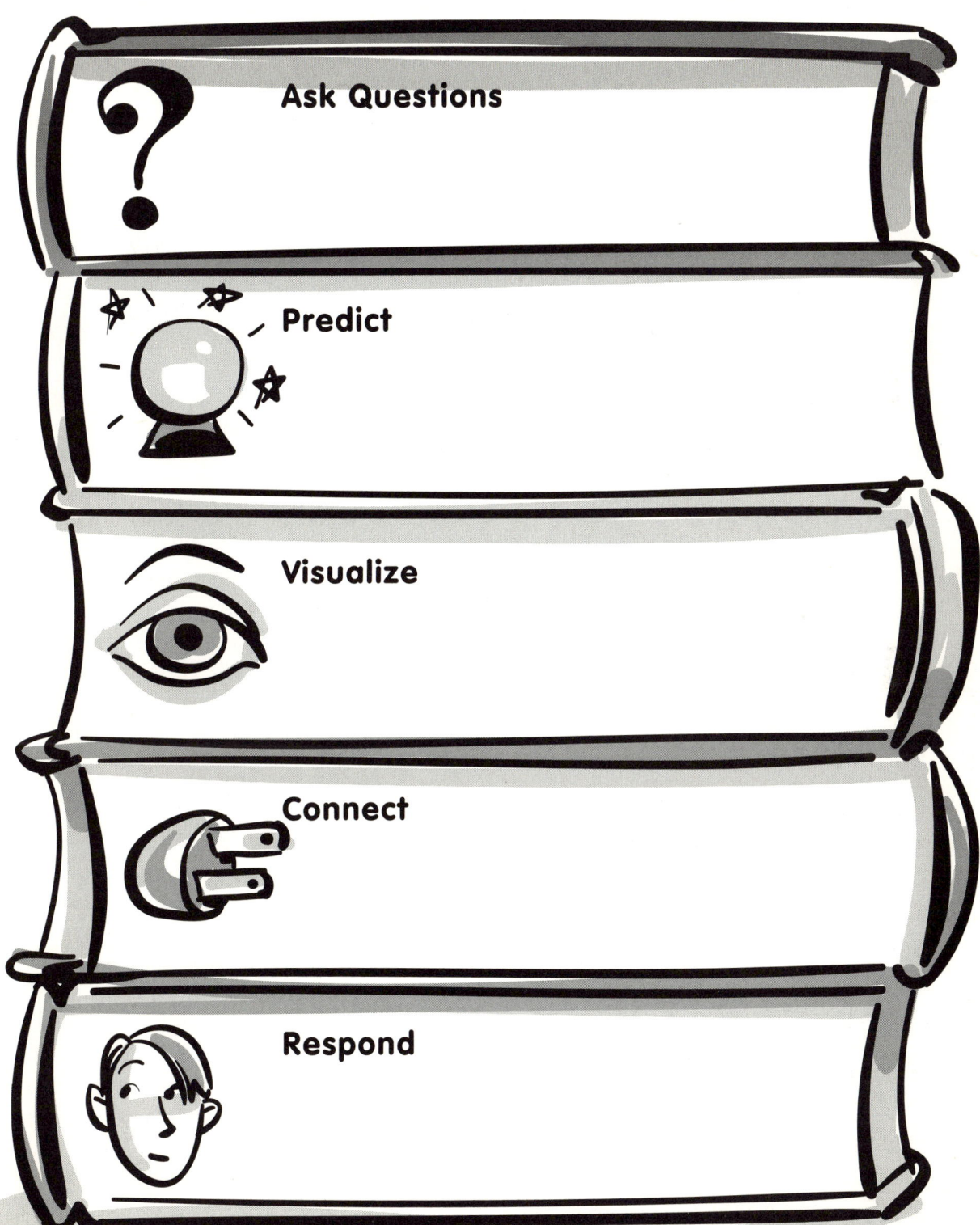

Teaching Guide: Powerful Predictions

Skills/Standards

- Uses clues to predict what happens next in a story
- Compares predictions with what actually happens in the story
- Revises predictions based on how the story progresses

Purpose

As they read, effective readers detect clues within the text and use them along with prior knowledge to make predictions about what will happen next. This graphic organizer assists students in making predictions as a way to comprehend the text better.

How to Use the Organizer

Select an exciting story to read. Mark places in the story where you would want students to stop and make predictions. Distribute copies of the Powerful Predictions graphic organizer (page 13) to each student and display a transparency copy on the overhead projector.

Read aloud the title, show illustrations, and review relevant sections to activate students' prior knowledge. Then read an opening portion of the story. Stop at a point where it makes sense for students to make a prediction. Ask: *What do you think will happen next?* As students make their predictions, have them explain what clues—whether from prior knowledge or from evidence in the text—led them to their predictions. Students should write the clues in the appropriate boxes and their prediction in the crystal ball.

Have students continue reading the story until they reach a place that indicates whether their prediction was on target or not. Instruct students to write what happened in the story in the boxes to the right of the crystal ball and compare their prediction with what actually happened in the story.

Connect the organizer and strategy to effective reading. Explain that proficient readers constantly make predictions about what will happen as they read. Provide guided and independent practice in making predictions to ensure that students utilize this strategy every time they read.

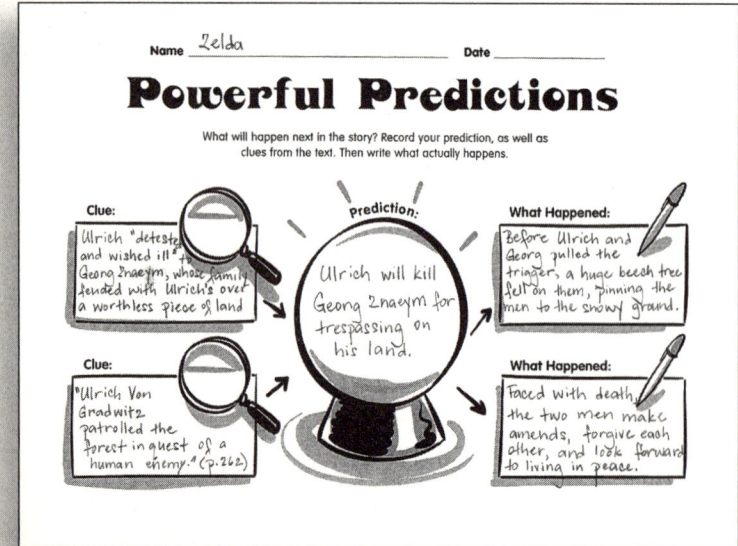

More to Do

As students continue to read a story, have them re-examine their predictions every so often. Ask: *Given what has happened so far in the story, does your original prediction still make sense?* If not, ask what new evidence in the story is causing them to rethink their prediction. Have them write this new evidence in the second clue box and their revised prediction below the crystal ball. Later, students should write what actually happened in the story and compare it to their revised prediction.

Name _____ Date _____

Powerful Predictions

What will happen next in the story? Record your prediction, as well as clues from the text. Then write what actually happens.

Keeping Track of Events

Teaching Guide

Skills/Standards
- Monitors own reading strategies and adjusts them as necessary
- Summarizes information in the text
- Questions whether or not the text makes sense

Purpose
Comprehending longer works of literature can be difficult for students. Often by the time they reach the end of a story, they have trouble remembering events from the beginning of the story. Summarizing the events and visualizing the characters, setting, and major conflicts in each chapter can aid in comprehension. Additionally, formulating questions helps the reader clarify information he or she did not understand.

How to Use the Organizer
Before students read a class- or self-selected novel, make booklets of the Keeping Track of Events organizer (page 15) for students. Photocopy one sheet for each chapter or section of the book, and staple the sheets together.

Introduce the graphic organizer to students by noting how sometimes it becomes difficult to keep track of events in a long book. Distribute the booklets to students and explain how the strategies in the organizer—summarizing, visualizing, and questioning—will help them become better readers. Model an example of a completed Keeping Track of Events organizer before letting students attempt to complete one on their own. Provide guided practice and give students an opportunity to complete an organizer in pairs or small groups prior to working independently.

Occasionally share examples of students' organizers. Encourage students to make suggestions for improvements and celebrate their strengths. Use students' questions as the basis for class and small group discussions.

More to Do
Modify the organizer and use it with expository text. Instead of summarizing events, have students summarize main ideas.

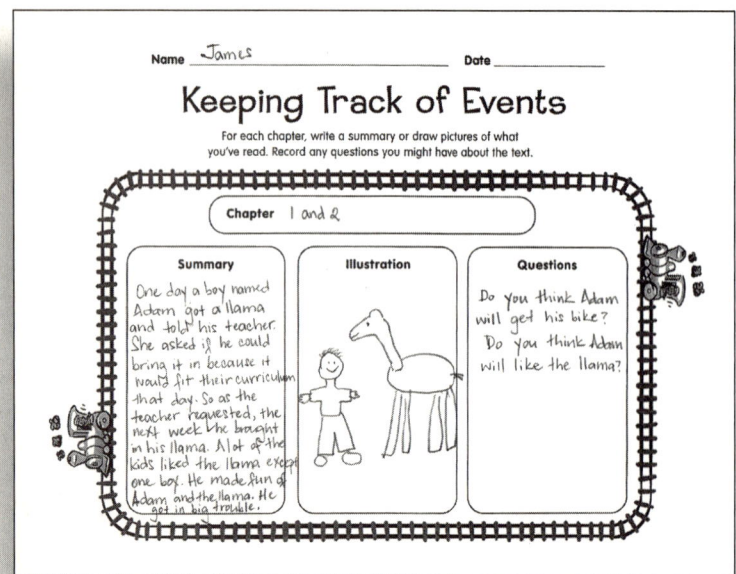

Name _____   Date _____

Keeping Track of Events

For each chapter, write a summary and draw pictures of what you've read. Record any questions you might have about the text.

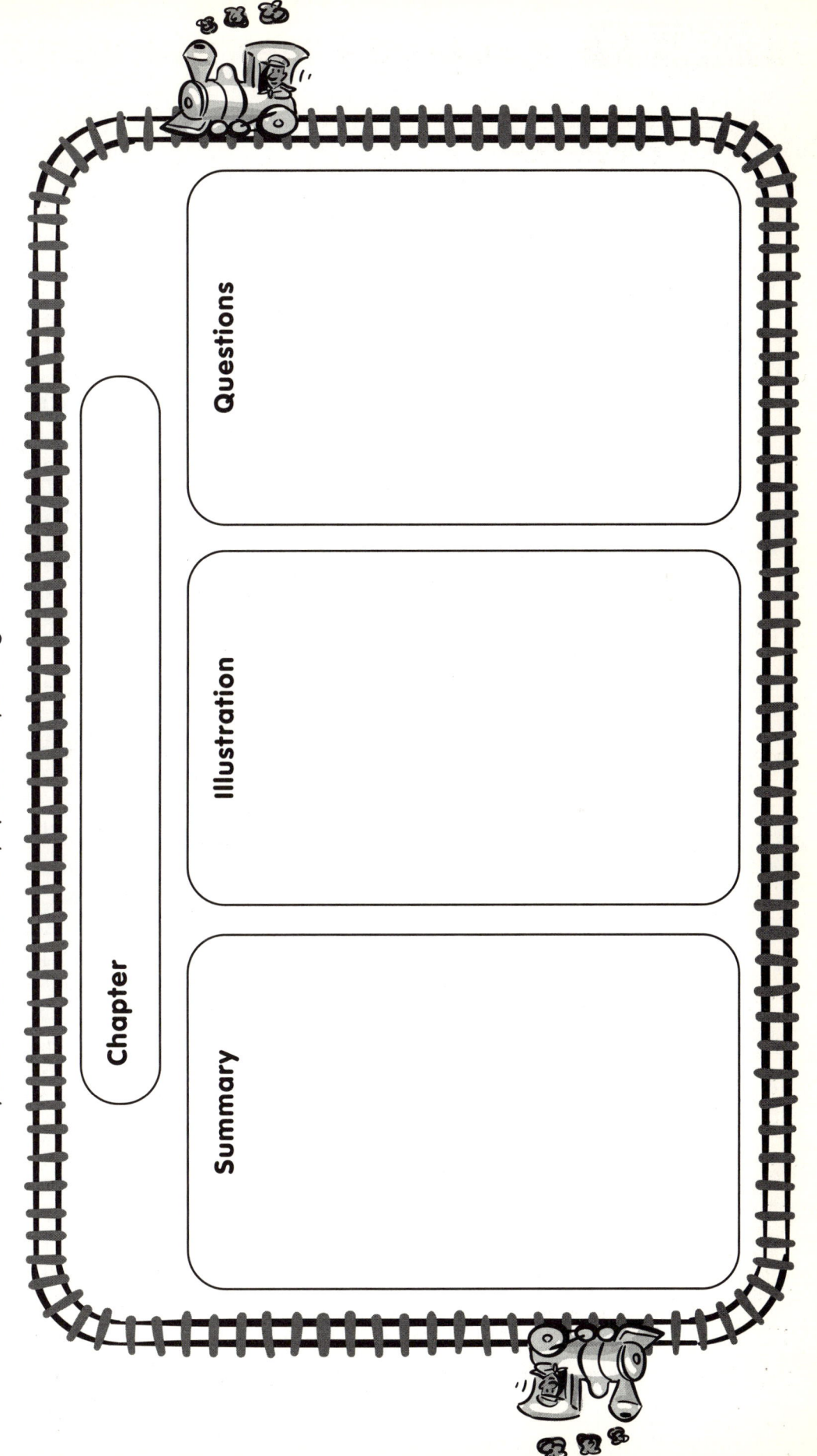

Chapter

Summary

Illustration

Questions

Reading & Writing Graphic Organizers & Mini-Lessons, page 15   Scholastic Teaching Resources

Teaching Guide: Questions for Discussion

Skills/Standards
- Generates questions about the text
- Reflects on and responds to questions
- Contributes to discussions about the text

Purpose
To spark meaningful discussions about a text or book, students need to generate questions that go beyond the literal level. Consequently, teaching students strategies for generating questions is imperative. This organizer assists students in formulating questions for literature discussion groups and summarizing the main points presented during the discussion.

How to Use the Organizer
Introduce students to the concept of big and small questions. Explain that "big questions" invite discussion; the answers are swirling in your head. On the other hand, "small questions" have a single answer that can be found easily in a book. Big questions start with *"What if…?" "Why do you think…?" "If you were ___, what would you have done when…?" "What was going through your head when…?" "What are some things that might happen next…?"* Small questions start with *"Who…?" "What…?" "Did…?" "How…?" "How many…?" "Where…?" "When…?"* Use a story the class has previously read to model examples of the two types of questions.

Read a short story aloud and ask students to think of big and small questions as they listen to the story. Distribute copies of the Questions for Discussion graphic organizer (page 17) to students. Have students write big questions and small questions in the appropriate spaces on their organizer.

Divide the class into small groups. Within their groups, ask students to share their questions, decide whether they are big or small, and justify the reason for their choice. Then have students use their questions as a springboard for discussing the story. Encourage students to jot down group members' responses to their questions as they come up during the discussion. Or, have students reflect on their own questions and write their response on the graphic organizer.

To prepare for future discussion groups, particularly of self-selected novels or stories, allow students to complete the organizer independently.

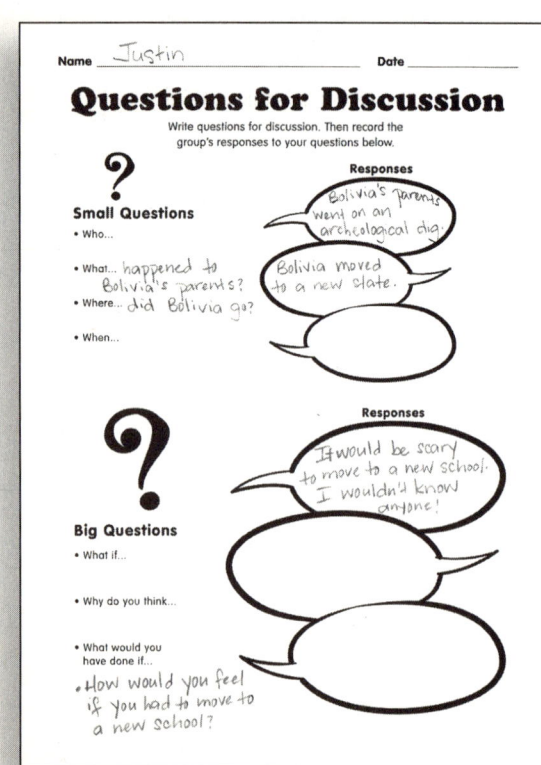

More to Do
Use the Questions for Discussion graphic organizer to generate questions about expository text and to summarize the main ideas.

Name _____   Date _____

Questions for Discussion

Write questions for discussion. Then record the group's responses to your questions below.

?

Small Questions

- Who...

- What...

- Where...

- When...

Responses

?

Big Questions

- What if...

- Why do you think...

- What would you have done if...

Responses

| Teaching Guide | # Character Portrait

> **Skills/Standards**
>
> - Understands elements of character development
> - Analyzes a character through his/her words, actions, appearance, and more

Purpose

To analyze and interpret a character, students need to examine the character's words, actions, thoughts, emotions, physical traits, and interaction with other characters. The purpose of this organizer is to familiarize students with the techniques an author uses to portray a character in order for them to understand this person or animal.

How to Use the Organizer

On the board, write the name of a character students are familiar with, such as Cinderella, Charlotte, or Wilbur. Ask students: *What can you say about this character?* List their responses on the board.

Explain that the responses on the board indicate how an author creates a character. Let students study the board for a few more minutes, instructing them to think about the different methods an author uses to portray a character—through the character's words, actions, thoughts, emotions, physical appearance, and interactions with other characters. Discuss students' responses and guide them to discover these six methods that an author uses to portray a character.

Distribute copies of the Character Portrait graphic organizer (page 19) to students. After students read a story, have them take direct quotes or evidence from the story and write them in the appropriate spaces to complete their Character Portrait. Instruct students to use direct quotes from the book when recording what the character says and what other characters say about the character.

More to Do

- Assign small groups different characters to analyze. Compare and contrast the different characters.
- Have students use Character Portrait as a prewriting organizer to create their own character or to write a character analysis.
- Ask students to read a biography and use the organizer to prepare an oral report about the famous person.

Name _____   Date _____

Character Portrait

Analyze a character by filling in the organizer below.

Starring _____

- What the character looks like
- What the character thinks
- What the character says
- What the character feels
- What other characters say about this character
- What the character does

Teaching Guide: Pleasing Plot

Skills/Standards

- Understands the basic concept of plot
- Identifies the different elements of plot, such as conflict, climax, and resolution

Purpose

This organizer provides students with the opportunity to explore the story element of plot. In addition, it helps students strengthen their recall of story events. It also serves as a precursor to developing the strategy of summarizing.

How to Use the Organizer

To introduce students to the concept of plot, draw a simple mountain-like plot diagram on the board. Next to the diagram, list the following terms: *initiating conflict, rising action, climax, falling action,* and *resolution.* Ask students: *How does this diagram relate to the plot of a story?* Guide them to label the diagram using the terms listed and ask if they can define each term.

Offer support if students need help with definitions. Explain that the term *initiating conflict* means "starting problem." *Rising action* refers to the events that lead to the *climax,* or the height of action in the story. *Falling action* includes events that happen after the climax, leading toward the *resolution.* Point out that the word *solution* is in the word *resolution* to help students make the connection that the resolution is the solution to the story problem. Remind them that stories do not always have a positive resolution and that some stories never resolve the problem.

Distribute copies of the Pleasing Plot graphic organizer (page 21) to students. Model how to use the organizer by reading a story together, then completing the plot diagram as a class through questioning and discussion. Move students through the continuum of direct instruction, guided practice, and independent practice by providing them with further opportunities to use the plot diagram.

More to Do

Use the diagram as a prewriting organizer to help students plan the plot for an original narrative, or have students use it to write a summary of the story.

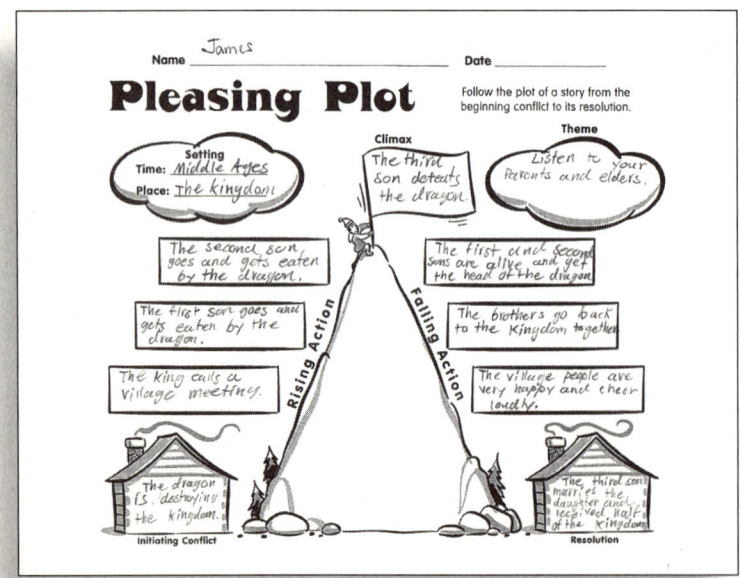

20 READING & WRITING GRAPHIC ORGANIZERS & MINI-LESSONS

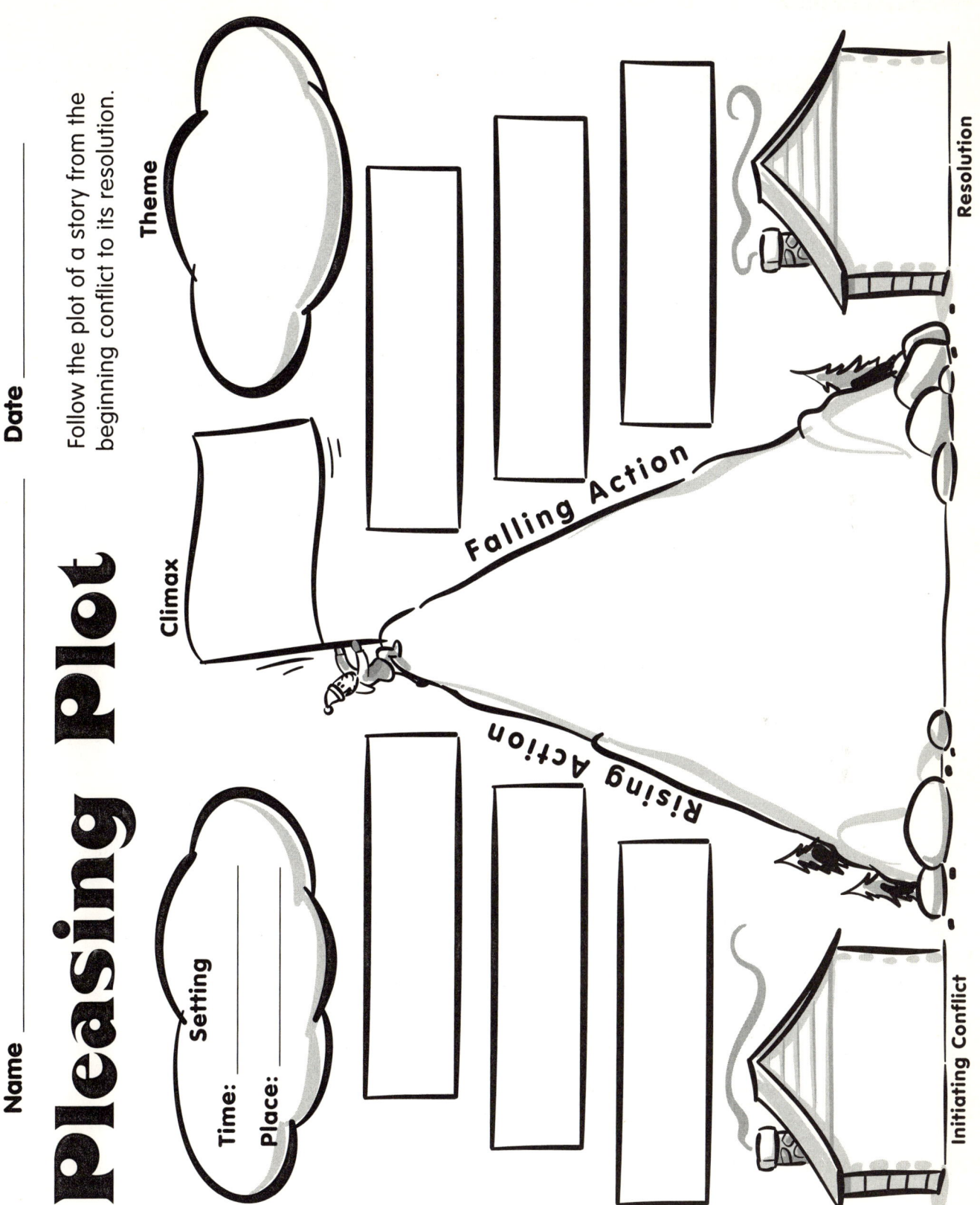

Teaching Guide: Super Sequence

Skills/Standards

- Orders events of a story or information in a text in sequence
- Summarizes and paraphrases information in a text
- Understands structural patterns or organization in informational text

Purpose

Use this graphic organizer to assist students in recalling the sequence of events in a story or in an informational text arranged in chronological order.

How to Use the Organizer

Read a story or an informational passage that has an obvious chronological order. Texts containing directions, procedures, or historical accounts are excellent choices.

Make an overhead transparency of the Super Sequence organizer (page 23). Distribute copies of the organizer and the story to students. Write the title of the story or article in the smoke cloud at the top of the organizer.

Divide the class into small groups. Instruct students to discuss the major events or ideas in the order that they appear in the text. Have students write the first event in the engine, the next event in the first car, and so on until they get to the final event in the caboose. As students identify the sequence of events, have them search for transition words that indicate chronological order, such as *first, next, later, then,* and *finally*. Ask students to write the transition word that connects one event to another above each car. Whenever the author omits the transition, have students provide one.

More to Do

- Use the organizer to plan an expository how-to paragraph or as a prewriting planner for giving directions, creating recipes, or outlining procedures. Students can also use Super Sequence to plan the order of events in an original narrative.

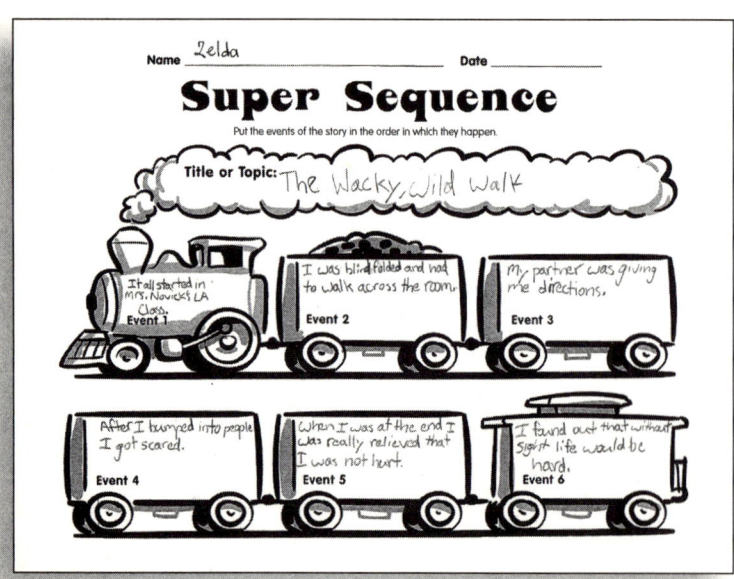

- Create a word wall or poster of transition words used to show chronological order. Encourage students to use these words to organize compositions arranged in chronological order and to identify this pattern of organization in a text.
- Allow visual learners to draw pictures of the events or ideas instead of writing them out in the cars. Encourage them to use a combination of writing and illustrations.

Name _____ Date _____

Super Sequence

Put the events of a story in the order in which they happen.

Title or Topic:

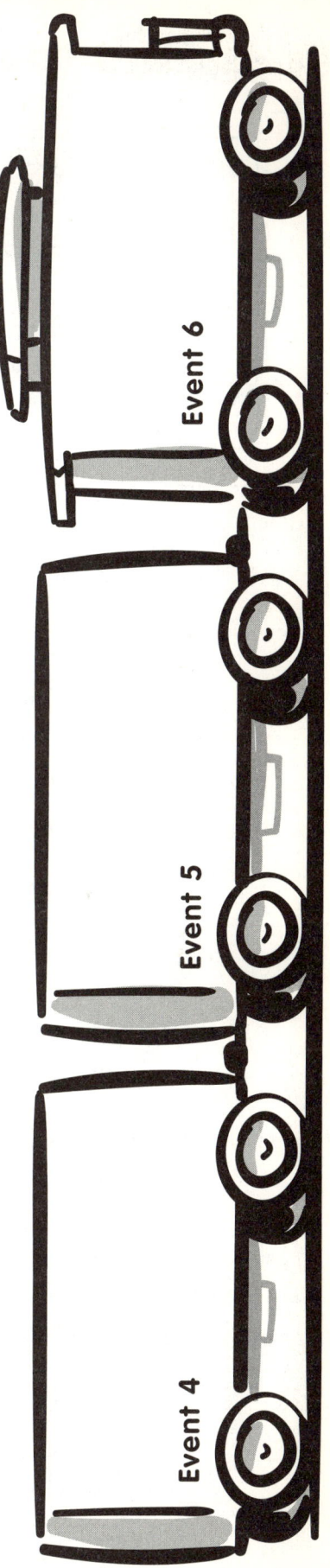

Event 1
Event 2
Event 3
Event 4
Event 5
Event 6

Teaching Guide: Main Event Bridge

Skills/Standards

- Identifies the main idea and supporting details in a text
- Uses text organizers to determine the main ideas and to locate information in a text

Purpose

To comprehend informational text, students need to search for information related to the author's purpose, method of organization, major ideas, and supporting details. This organizer is designed to help students focus on these essential elements of informational text to improve their comprehension.

How to Use the Organizer

Select an informational text that uses chronological order or enumeration as the method of organization. Before reading, list these questions on the board:

- What is the author's purpose or reason for writing this?
- What is the main idea of the passage?
- What details does the author use to support and develop the main idea?

Explain to students that focusing on these questions as they read informational text will help them improve comprehension. Distribute copies of the Main Event Bridge graphic organizer (page 25) to students.

Read the text aloud, instructing students to listen carefully to find the answers to the questions above. Discuss students' answers, then have them fill in the appropriate sections in the organizer.

More to Do

- Use the organizer as a prewriting strategy for expository paragraphs.
- Modify the organizer to encompass two or three main ideas and their supporting details.
- Have students complete the organizer after listening to an oral presentation to assess their understanding of the information presented.

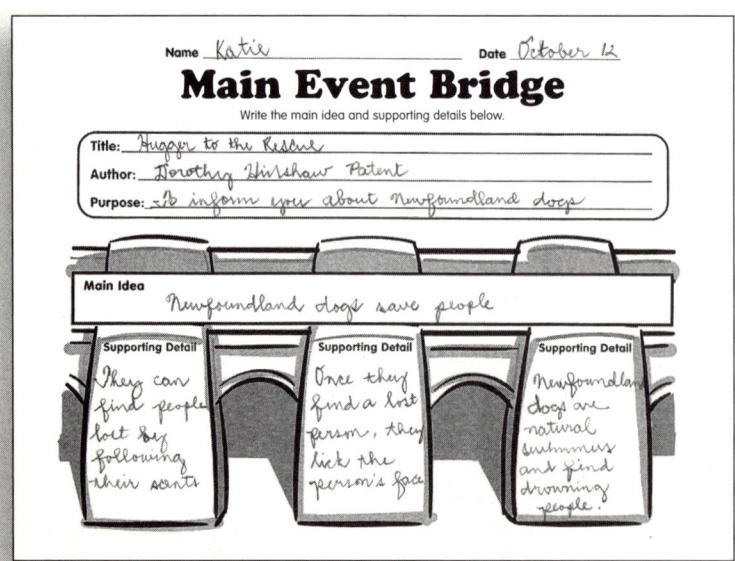

Name _____ Date _____

Main Event Bridge

Write the main idea and supporting details below.

Title:
Author:
Purpose:

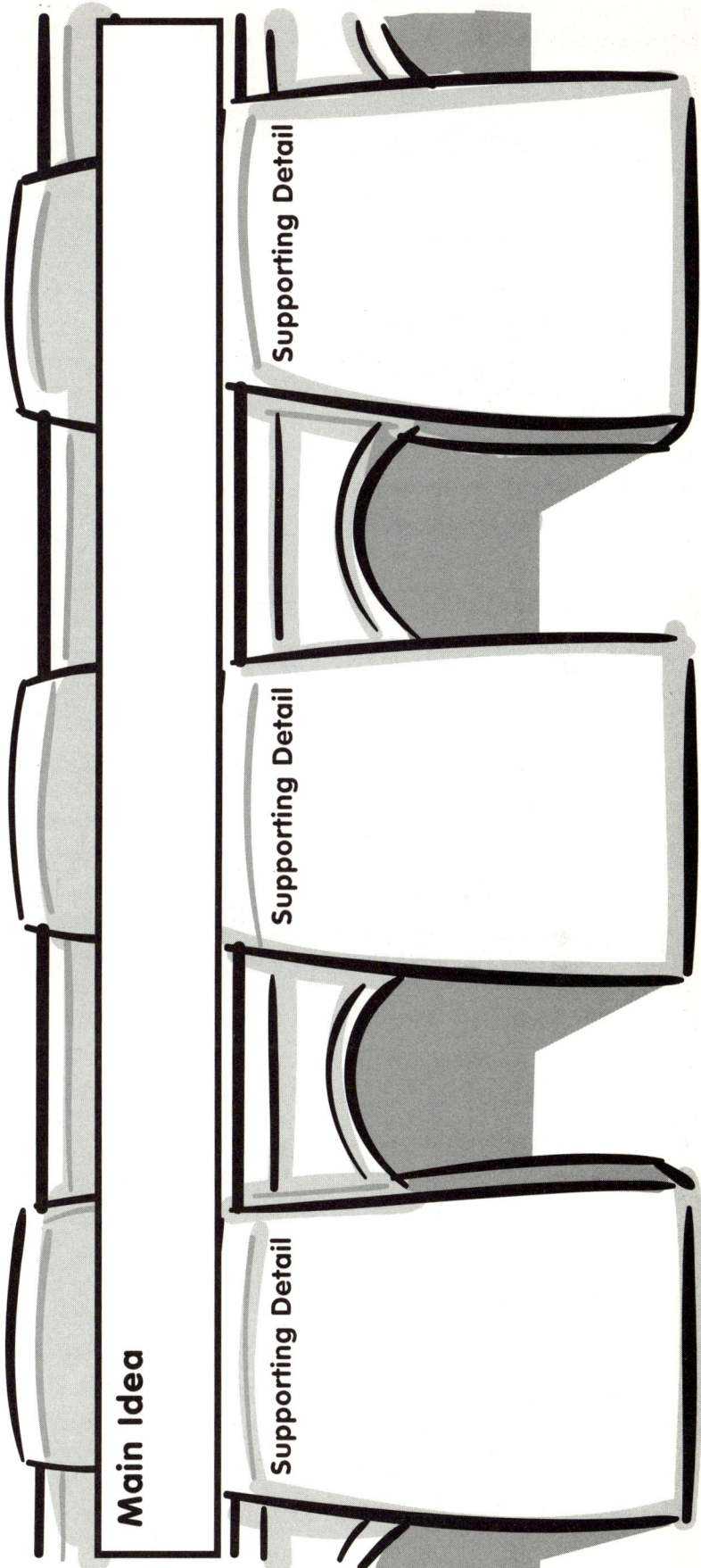

Main Idea

Supporting Detail

Supporting Detail

Supporting Detail

Teaching Guide
Cause and Effect

Skills/Standards
- Identifies cause and effect
- Understands cause-and-effect relationships

Purpose
In a story, the cause is the reason why something happens, and the effect is what happens as a result. Comprehension improves when readers recognize the connections between causes and effects. Consequently, this organizer assists students in identifying and analyzing causes and effects in stories.

How to Use the Organizer
If possible, use a plastic bowling set to physically model cause-effect. Have students take turns bowling. Ask the class why some pins fall down while others stay up. Connect the word *why* to the cause. The bowling ball is the reason (the cause) why the pins fall down. The pins fall down as a result of the ball hitting them. Transfer this concept to a story. What happens in a story is the *effect* or result. Why it happens is the *cause*.

After reading a story aloud, ask students to identify some events that happen in the story. Write some of their responses on the board. Next, have students examine the events on the board and provide a reason why some of the events happened. Write the student-generated cause-effect relationships on the board. Clearly label the cause and the effect. Throughout the discussion, encourage students to look for a cause that creates multiple effects and for effects that have multiple causes. Illustrate multiple causes and multiple effects on the board to demonstrate the variety and complexity of cause-effect relationships.

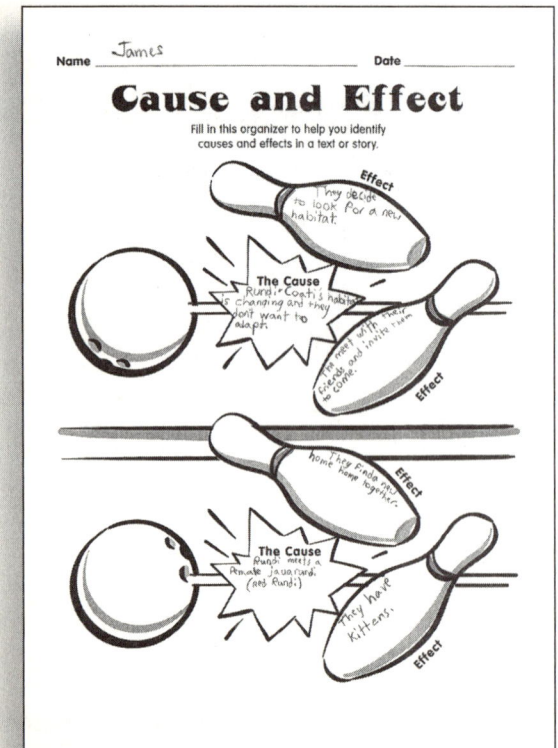

Distribute the Cause and Effect organizer (page 27) to students. Have students work with partners or in small groups to identify additional cause-effect relationships in the story. Suggest, for example, that students examine a character's motive. Why does the character take a specific action? What is the effect of his/her action?

As a whole class, discuss the various groups' causes and effects. Point out similarities and differences.

More to Do
Use the organizer to assist students in understanding the cause-effect pattern in informational text. Direct students to identify signal words such as *for this reason*, *therefore*, and *as a result*.

Name _____   Date _____

Cause and Effect

Fill in this organizer to help you identify
causes and effects in a text or story.

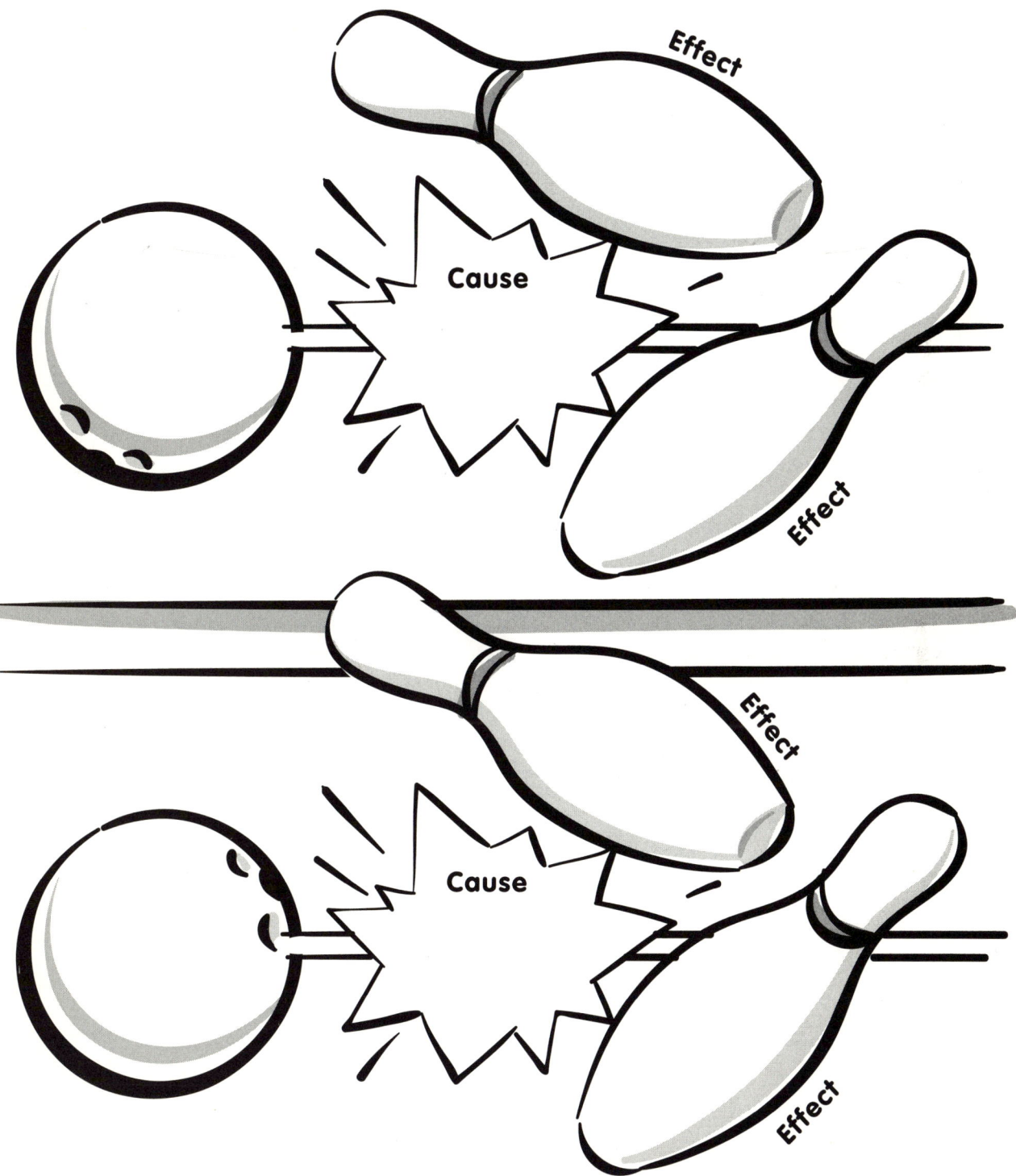

Teaching Guide → Blueprint for a Paragraph

Skills/Standards

- Uses prewriting strategies to plan written work
- Identifies parts of a paragraph
- Plans and organizes a paragraph

Purpose

Prewriting is a critical component of the writing process. This organizer helps students review the elements of a paragraph and plan a how-to or sequential paragraph.

How to Use the Organizer

Review the different parts of a paragraph: the topic sentence, supporting details, and the closing, or clincher, sentence. Ask students to think about how a house might be similar to a paragraph. Discuss how the roof encompasses or covers a house, similar to how a topic sentence encompasses a paragraph by telling what the paragraph will be about. The different floors of a house (first, second, and maybe third) hold up or support the roof, just like supporting details in a paragraph support the topic sentence. The clincher sentence reinforces the paragraph, just like the basement acts as a foundation for the house.

Make an overhead transparency of the Blueprint for a Paragraph graphic organizer (page 29) and distribute photocopies to students. Using the think-aloud strategy, model how to write a how-to paragraph step by step. For example, as you write the topic sentence, remind students that this sentence states the main idea and grabs the reader's attention.

After you write your own topic sentence on the overhead, encourage students to choose what they will write about. List some of their suggested topics on the board and provide time for students to construct and share some of their topic sentences. Continue this process of defining, modeling, writing, and sharing until students complete the organizer.

Before students write the supporting details and the clincher, point out that just as stairs connect one floor of a house to another, transition words, such as *first* and *next*, connect one supporting detail to another. Finally, emphasize that the clincher sentence summarizes the main idea and differs from the topic sentence.

Have students use the organizer to compose their rough draft.

More to Do

Change the transition words on the stairs to teach students different patterns for organizing paragraphs. For example, if students are writing about similarities between two things, place words such as *similarly*, *also*, and *like* on the stairs.

Name _____ Date _____

Blueprint for a Paragraph

Before you write, plan your story with this graphic organizer.

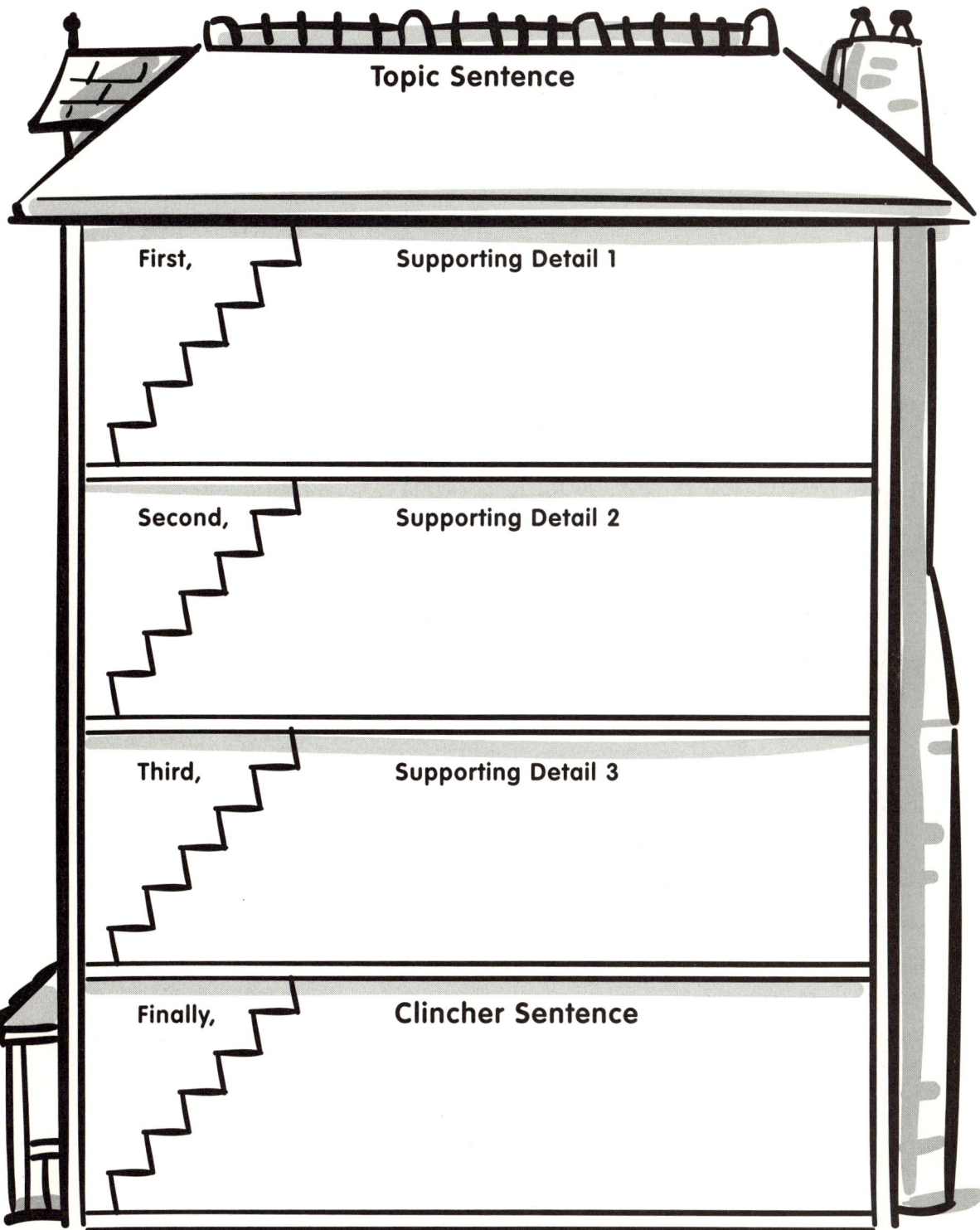

Teaching Guide: Satisfying Senses

Skills/Standards
- Brainstorms sensory words to use in writing
- Uses descriptive language

Purpose
To write effective, descriptive poems or paragraphs and to add powerful sensory language to stories, students need to employ words associated with the five senses. This organizer stimulates students to brainstorm specific language and imagery that leads to powerful writing.

How to Use the Organizer
Create sensory shoeboxes to stimulate students' senses. Make and label "see," "feel," "smell," and "hear" boxes. Inside each box place objects related to the appropriate sense. For example, put a maraca, jingle bell, and small pair of cymbals in the "hear" box. Instead of a taste box, fill individual sandwich bags with a piece of candy, pretzel, fruit chewy, and other items students can eat safely.

Divide the class into groups of four. Outline clear rules for the use of the boxes, such as, "One person touches at a time." Distribute one box per group and a copy of the Satisfying Senses graphic organizer (page 31) to each student. Explain to students that as they examine the items in the boxes, they should record words that describe their sensory experiences in the appropriate spaces on the organizer. For example, they should write "see" words next to the eye and "smell" words next to the nose. Encourage students to use powerful, unique words, such as *scarlet* instead of *red* for a "see" word and *pungent* instead of *strong* for a "smell" word. On your signal, have students exchange boxes until each group has brainstormed words related to each sense.

Write the words on sentence strips and use them to create a Sensory Word Wall that students can refer to each time they write. Add new ones throughout the year.

More to Do
Do a guided imagery that stimulates students' senses. For example, simulate a trip to the beach in the classroom. Play a recording of ocean sounds, spread beach towels on the floor, fill boxes with sand and shells, and spread pictures of beach scenes and stuffed sea animals everywhere. As you take students on a mental journey, have them record what they see, hear, feel, touch, and taste. Invite them to use the experience to create poems or descriptive paragraphs.

Name _____ Date _____

Satisfying Senses

List describing words that stimulate each of your senses.
Use these words for more descriptive writing.

See Words

_____
_____
_____
_____

Smell Words

_____
_____
_____
_____

Sound Words

_____
_____
_____
_____

Taste Words

_____
_____
_____
_____

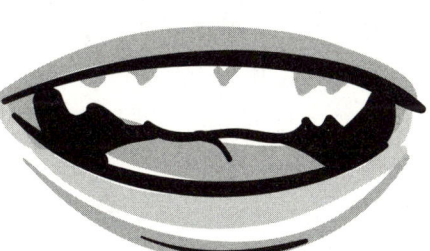

Touch Words

_____
_____
_____
_____

Teaching Guide: Nifty Narrative

Skills/Standards

- Selects a topic for narrative writing
- Creates an organized structure for the narrative
- Uses sensory details to enhance story

Purpose

This organizer assists students with writing a personal narrative about a special memory or event in their lives. The organizer is designed to help students add rich detail to their narratives to make stories come alive for the reader.

How to Use the Organizer

Read Sandra Cisneros's short story "Eleven" or another narrative that completely engages the reader in the writer's personal experience. Discuss the techniques and the language the author uses to make the event compelling and memorable.

As a class, brainstorm topics for students' personal narratives. If possible, have students collect objects or photos or create a personal time line to help them recall an important experience or event in their lives. Distribute copies of the Nifty Narrative graphic organizer (page 33). Ask students to select their topic and write it on the organizer.

Emphasize the need to include strong sensory language and emotions in the narrative to avoid "bare bones" writing that makes the reader fall asleep. Have students write the feelings and emotions surrounding the memory inside the oval with the faces near it. Ask them to visualize what they saw, heard, smelled, tasted, and touched during their experience and to list these sensory images inside the oval near the eye, nose, and mouth.

Model a completed organizer for students and show them how to use it to draft a narrative. The transition from the organizer to the draft will be most effective if you compose your own narrative and show how the organizer relates to what you have written. Have students use the organizer to write the drafts of their stories.

More to Do

Individually or in small groups have students use the organizer to analyze an author's personal narrative. Or ask students to become a character in a story and create a personal narrative from that character's point of view.

Name _____ Date _____

Nifty Narrative

Use this organizer to plan your personal narrative. What are the main events? How did you feel as they happened? What sensory details can you add?

Topic _____

Teaching Guide: Perfectly Persuasive

Skills/Standards

- Selects a topic for persuasive writing
- Identifies position regarding the topic
- Generates reasons and facts to support position

Purpose

This organizer develops students' persuasive writing skills and assists them in composing persuasive essays or letters to the editor.

How to Use the Organizer

Write the word *persuade* on the board and ask students to define it. Ask them to give examples of situations in which they had to convince their parents or another person to do something. Have students consider how they might use writing as a persuasive tool. Ask: *What kind of persuasive writing have you seen in the real world?* Discuss different kinds of persuasive writing—advertisements, editorials, political speeches—and make a list of techniques authors use to persuade prospective buyers or voters.

Brainstorm a list of noncontroversial topics that students have strong opinions about, such as year-round school, uniforms, or skateboarding in public places. Choose one topic and ask students to pick a position (for or against) regarding this topic. Display a transparency copy of the Perfectly Persuasive graphic organizer (page 35) on the overhead projector, and distribute photocopies to students. Write the topic and students' position at the top of the organizer. Next, ask students to think of some reasons that support their position. Encourage them to come up with concrete facts to back up each reason. For example, if the topic is school uniforms and their position is "for" it, students might point out how much money is spent buying new clothes each year. List students' reasons on the board, then pick the three most persuasive points. Finally, discuss how students might conclude the piece.

Divide the class into small groups, putting together students who are interested in the same topic and have similar positions to complete their organizers. Individually or in small groups, have students compose persuasive essays or letters about their topics, writing to an authentic audience such as the school board or local newspaper when possible. Explain that their introductions should clearly state the topic and their position. The body should contain three reasons for the position, along with facts and examples that firmly support each one. Finally, the conclusion should restate the position and summarize the reasons for it in a powerful new way.

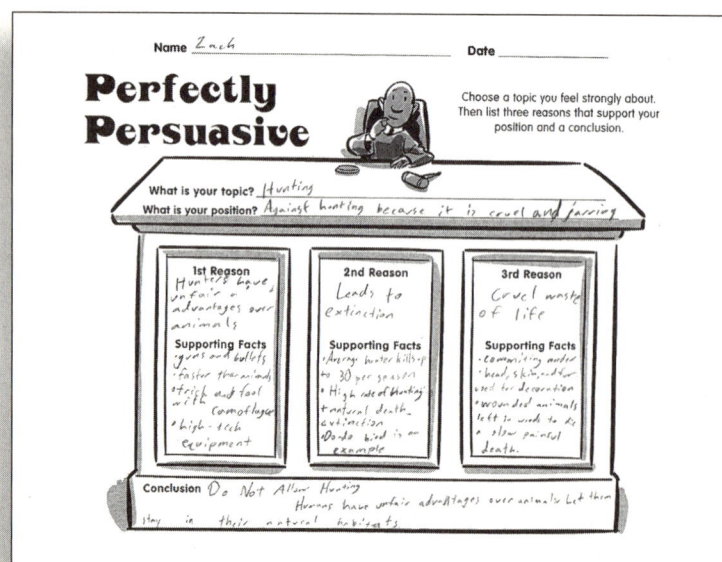

34 READING & WRITING GRAPHIC ORGANIZERS & MINI-LESSONS

Name _____   Date _____

Perfectly Persuasive

Choose a topic you feel strongly about. List three reasons that support your position and then state a conclusion.

What is your topic? _____

What is your position? _____

1st Reason	2nd Reason	3rd Reason
Supporting Facts	Supporting Facts	Supporting Facts

Conclusion

Teaching Guide: Excellent Essay

Skills/Standards

- Plans a three-paragraph essay
- Orders ideas in logical sequence
- Writes a conclusion that ties together the ideas

Purpose

Communication skills involve reading, writing, speaking, and listening. To communicate ideas and information effectively, students must learn to write multiparagraph papers. This organizer guides students through the process.

How to Use the Organizer

Share with students an example of a well-written three-paragraph essay. Read the essay aloud and discuss its various components. Ask students to identify the main idea statement in the introduction and the transition words. As students discover the elements present in the introduction, body, and conclusion, list them on chart paper or on the board and have students record these notes. Make the investigation more interesting by designing a simple scavenger hunt to help students extract the information.

Distribute copies of the Excellent Essay graphic organizer (page 37) to students. Let students choose a topic to write about or assign one. In the space labeled "Introduction," have students construct a three- to five-sentence introductory paragraph. Refer them to the reminder statements on the spoons as they work on their introduction.

Next, have students compose the body of the essay on the three scoops of ice cream. Point out that each detail should relate back to the ideas outlined in the introduction. Instruct students to write the conclusion inside the sundae dish. Remind students that the conclusion restates the main idea and summarizes the main points of the body paragraph.

Finally, have students use the graphic organizer to draft their three-paragraph essay.

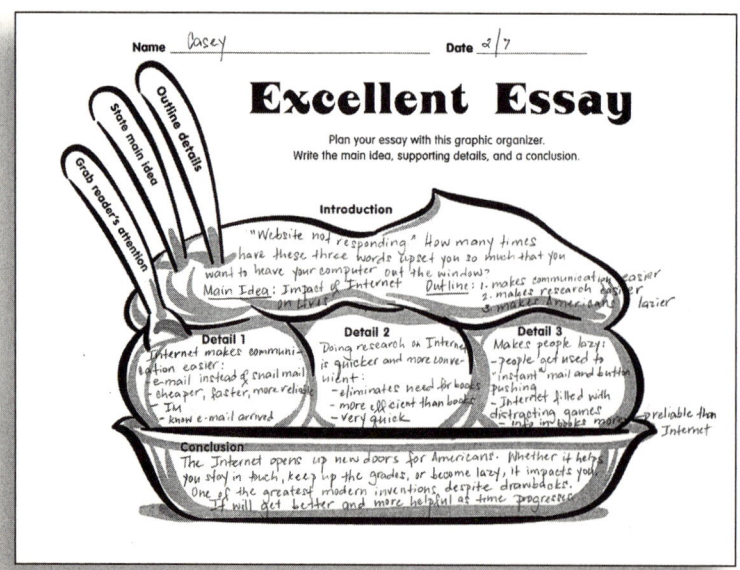

More to Do

Older students can use this organizer to compose a five-paragraph essay. Each scoop of ice cream becomes a separate paragraph. The organizer provides excellent practice for state writing assessments, too.

Name _____ Date _____

Excellent Essay

Plan your essay with this graphic organizer.
Write the main idea, supporting details, and a conclusion.

- Grab reader's attention
- State main idea
- Outline details

Introduction

Detail 1

Detail 2

Detail 3

Conclusion

Teaching Guide: Spectacular Story

Skills/Standards
- Identifies story elements
- Develops characters, setting, and plot
- Establishes conflict and creates a satisfying resolution

Purpose
When creating an original narrative, many students simply write the plot. They forget to begin with a well-defined problem, embellish the characters and setting, use dialogue, and add figurative language. This organizer helps students effectively plan their stories.

How to Use the Organizer
As students read stories throughout the year, engage them in several discussions about what makes stories memorable. Provide numerous models before asking students to attempt to write their own stories.

Display a transparency copy of the Spectacular Story graphic organizer (page 39) on the overhead projector and distribute photocopies to students. Tell students that they will be writing a piece of original fiction. To engage the reader, writers need to create an interesting, powerful story problem. Ask students to suggest conflicts, and list their responses on the board. After students decide on a conflict, have them write it on the space labeled "Problem" on the organizer. Next, ask them to imagine two characters engaged in this conflict. Choose one of the story problems listed on the board to model how to create characters that fit the conflict. Then have students develop their own characters and record the information on their organizer.

Discuss how setting can enhance the tone and mood of a story. Again, use one of the class story problems to model effective settings before inviting students to choose theirs. Continue this process of discussing, modeling, and completing the organizer for the other story elements. Suggest that students determine the resolution to the story before deciding on the events; this makes the events easier to write.

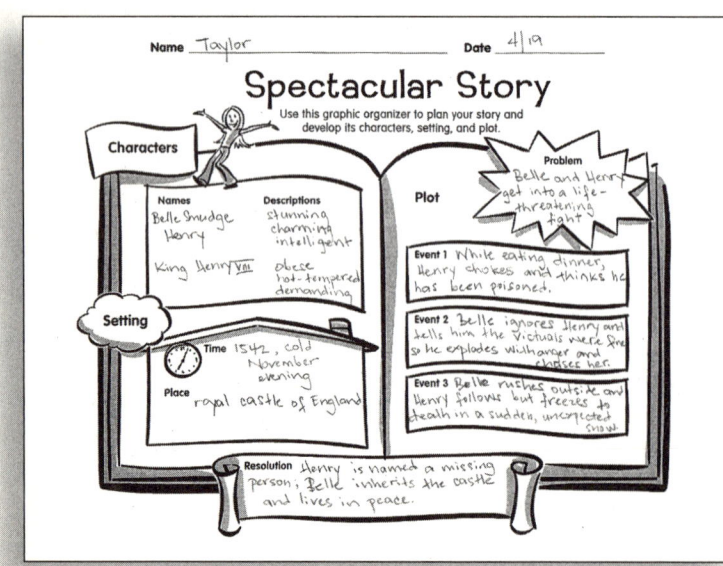

As students draft their stories, remind them to include a brief description of the characters, setting, and story problem in the introduction. Show them how to use dialogue to communicate the events and enhance the conflict.

More to Do
Have partners or small groups work together to create a Spectacular Story map and use it to create a script for a play or puppet show. Each member of the group becomes a character and recites his or her lines for the performance.

Teaching Guide: Sensational Summary

Skills/Standards
- Identifies story elements
- Summarizes and paraphrases main idea and other details in text

Purpose
An effective after-reading strategy is summarizing, which is a difficult skill because it involves the ability to interpret the text and write or paraphrase that information concisely. This organizer guides students through the process of writing a one-paragraph, short-story summary.

How to Use the Organizer
Explain to students the characteristics of an effective summary: It is brief, describes the main topic or theme, includes only important information, organizes the ideas clearly, and restates the major points in their own words.

Read a simple story such as a fable or folk tale with the class. Distribute copies of the Sensational Summary graphic organizer (page 41) to students. Using an overhead transparency of the organizer, lead the class through the process of gathering information for the summary. First, explain that the topic sentence includes the title, author, and main idea, which usually relates to the story problem or major conflict. As you fill in this information in the Topic Sentence section of the transparency, have students record it on their organizer as well.

Continue the process of discussing the ingredients for the supporting details and clincher sentence and complete each section on the organizer with the class's assistance.

Next, use the graphic organizer to draft a one-paragraph summary on chart paper. As you model the process, think aloud so that students see the connection between the organizer and the paragraph. As you add each item from the organizer, check it off in the box provided. Allow students to help you with the writing process.

Provide students with guided practice before they independently complete an organizer and write a summary.

More to Do
Show examples of effective and not-so effective summaries. Ask students which ones are better and why. Have students suggest revisions for the not-so-effective summaries and then apply the revision techniques to their own summaries.

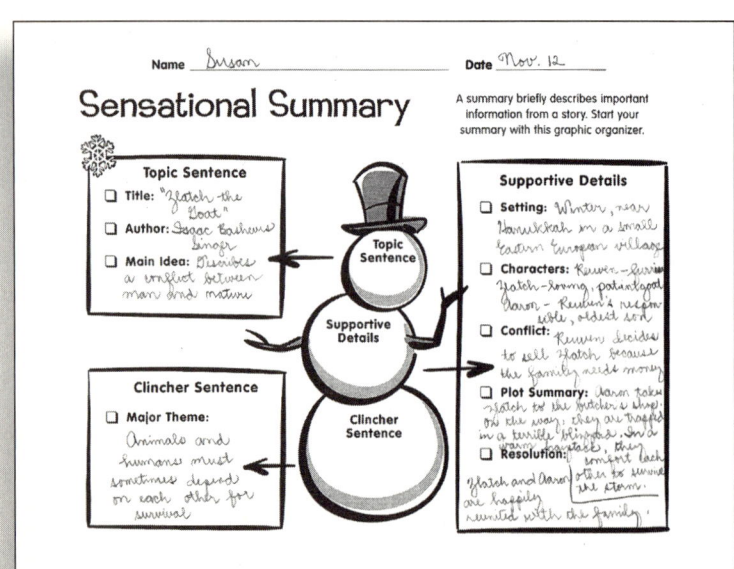

40 READING & WRITING GRAPHIC ORGANIZERS & MINI-LESSONS

Name _____ Date _____

Sensational Summary

A summary briefly describes important information from a story. Start your summary with this graphic organizer.

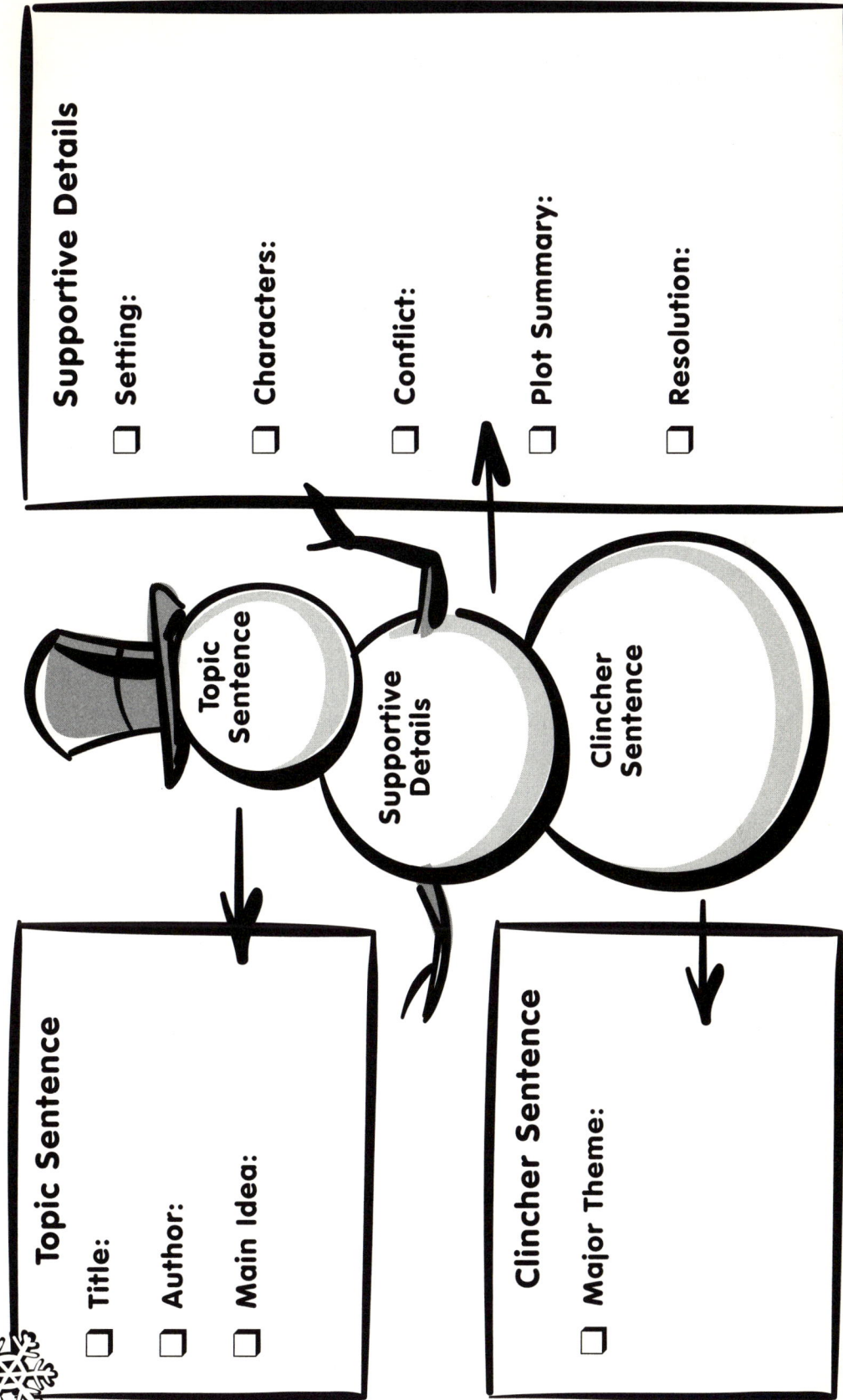

Supportive Details

- ☐ Setting:
- ☐ Characters:
- ☐ Conflict:
- ☐ Plot Summary:
- ☐ Resolution:

Topic Sentence

- ☐ Title:
- ☐ Author:
- ☐ Main Idea:

Clincher Sentence

- ☐ Major Theme:

Reading & Writing Graphic Organizers & Mini-Lessons, page 41   Scholastic Teaching Resources

Teaching Guide: Compare-Contrast Matrix

Skills/Standards

- Identifies similarities and differences between two topics
- Decides on criteria for comparing topics

Purpose

The Compare-Contrast Matrix is used to represent information that is being compared and/or contrasted. Major ideas related to the topics being compared are listed and analyzed. Encourage students to use the matrix as a prewriting strategy for organizing a comparative paragraph or paper.

How to Use the Organizer

Distribute photocopies of the Compare-Contrast Matrix (page 43) to students. Explain that this graphic organizer is helpful in finding similarities and differences between two topics, the first step in writing a comparative paper.

Use a transparency copy of the graphic organizer to model how to complete it. First, identify the topics being compared and instruct students to write them next to Topic 1 and Topic 2 on the organizer (for example, George Washington and Abraham Lincoln). Next, list the major ideas related to the topics in the Major Idea column and have students record them (their childhood, education, and presidency). Discuss each major idea's relationship to Topic 1 and Topic 2. Record the information in the appropriate columns.

Use the completed organizer to model how to write a compare-contrast paragraph or essay. Teach students how to incorporate transition words, such as *similarly*, *in the same way*, *in contrast*, or *on the other hand*, into the paragraph. Justify your choices and explain why specific transition words are important.

Assign or let students choose topics for a comparison paper. Have them complete a Compare-Contrast Matrix before drafting the paper.

More to Do

- To provide background knowledge necessary for students to understand a comparative expository text, prepare a completed Compare-Contrast Matrix for students before reading the text. Have students write a comparative paragraph that incorporates the information on the organizer. During and after reading, discuss similarities and differences between students' paragraphs and the text.
- When reading historical fiction, have students use the organizer to compare the novel's time period to the present.

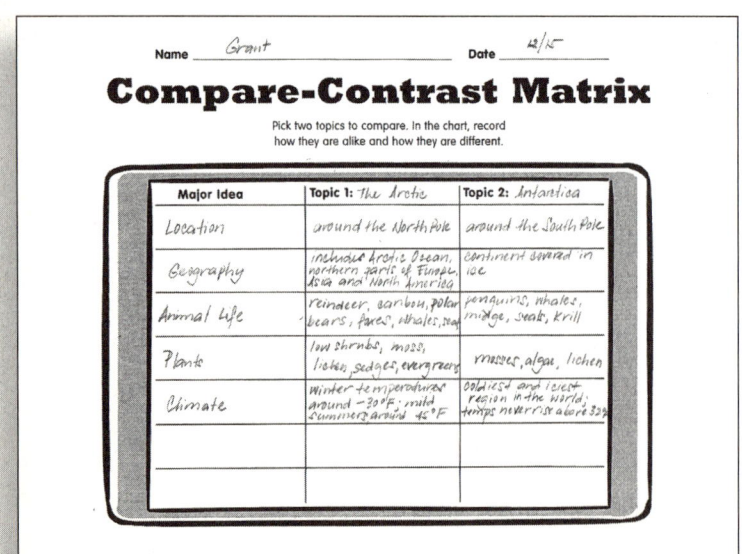

Name _____ Date _____

Compare-Contrast Matrix

Pick two topics to compare. In the chart, record how they are alike and how they are different.

Major Idea	Topic 1:	Topic 2:

Teaching Guide: Neat Notes for Research

Skills/Standards

- Generates questions for research
- Gathers and records information for research
- Synthesizes information to write a report

Purpose

Research literally means "to search again." To conduct this search, students must generate questions about their topics, read to find answers to their questions, and record the information they find. The purpose of this organizer is to help students gather information about a research topic.

How to Use the Organizer

Distribute copies of the Neat Notes graphic organizer (page 45) to students. Assign topics related to a unit of study or allow students to choose a topic to research. Evaluate each student's topic, then have him or her write the topic at the top of the organizer.

Model how to generate meaningful questions about a topic. Explain to students that questions such as, *How is Mars similar to Earth?* or *What are some of Mars's major landforms?* are good questions because they are neither too broad nor too narrow. However, questions such as, *How many moons does Mars have?* or *What are all of Mars's characteristics?* are not effective because the first is too narrow and the other is too broad. Have students think of four questions about their topic.

After reviewing students' questions, tell them to record one question in each section on the organizer. Explain that they may need to form new questions or modify the old ones based on the information they locate. Students may need more than one copy of the organizer to gather information.

Using their own words and short, meaningful phrases (model this first), students should record the information they find in the appropriate section. Make sure they note their sources for the information they find.

To write a paper about the topic, students can change each question into a statement to form a topic sentence for each paragraph. The information in the box becomes the supportive details.

More to Do

Teach students the SQ3R (survey, question, read, recite, review) method of studying an expository chapter in a textbook. After surveying the text, students write questions about the chapter on the organizer and then record (recite) their answers to the questions after reading.

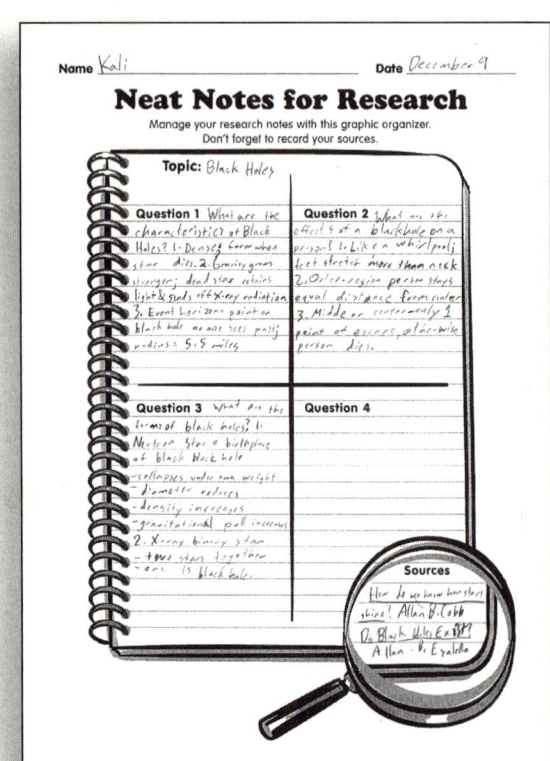

Name _____   Date _____

Neat Notes for Research

Manage your research notes with this graphic organizer.
Don't forget to record your sources.

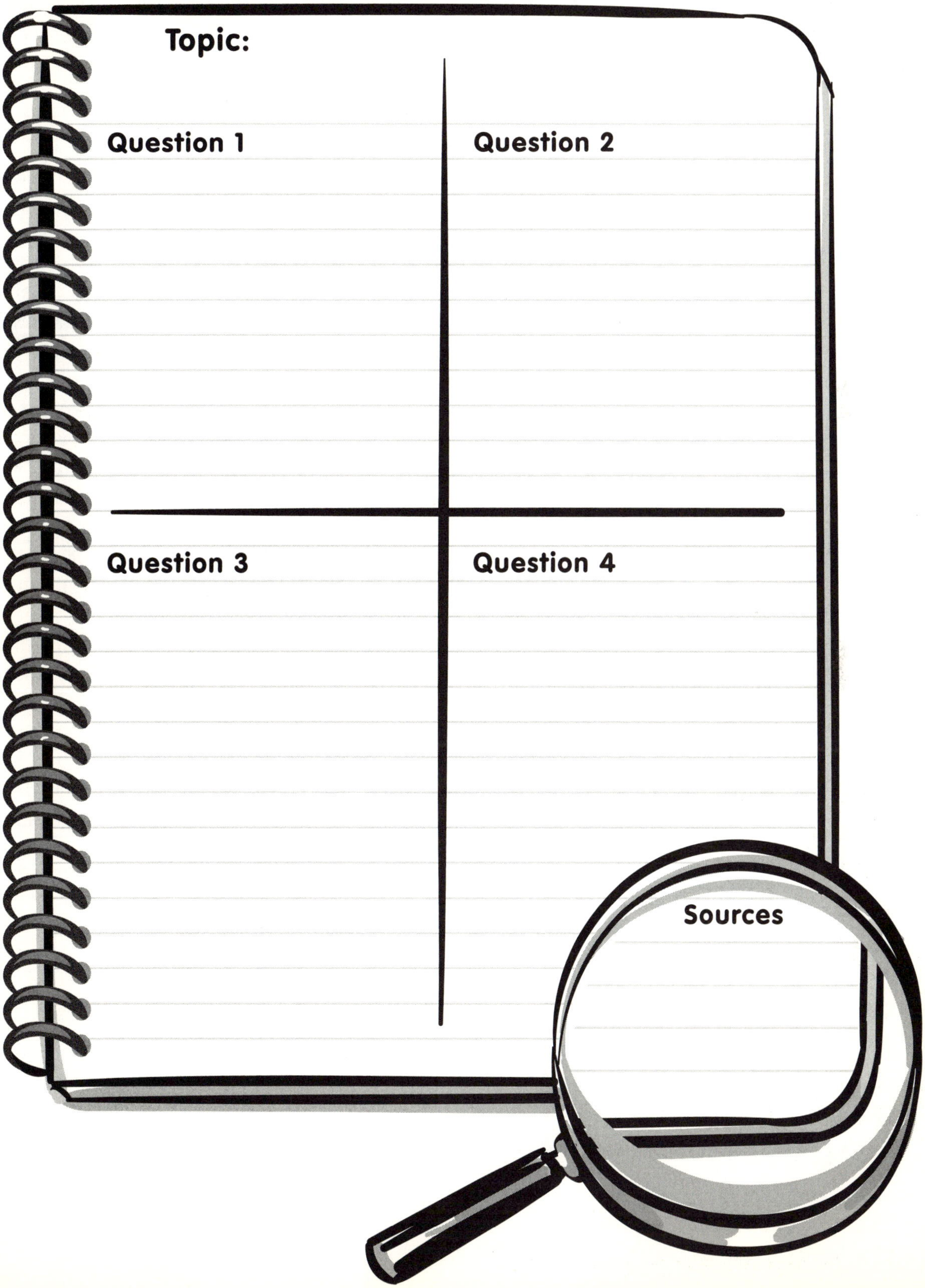

Topic:

Question 1

Question 2

Question 3

Question 4

Sources

Teaching Guide: Simply Sources

Skills/Standards

- Uses a variety of sources to gather information
- Cites information about sources

Purpose

Correctly citing sources is an essential part of any research process. Use this organizer to help students collect correct data for each source. Recording the information in the manner suggested on the Simply Sources organizer simplifies the transition to an MLA-style bibliography.

How to Use the Organizer

Display a transparency copy of the Simply Sources graphic organizer (page 47) on the overhead projector. Explain to students that when conducting research, they need to list their sources and cite them in a bibliography. Using a book, encyclopedia, magazine article, and Web site, demonstrate how to locate the author or editor's name, the title, city, publisher, date, volume number, Web address, and other relevant information. Record the information on the transparency.

Divide the class into small groups. Provide each group with a book, an encyclopedia, and a Web site article, and distribute a copy of the graphic organizer to each student. Ask students to examine one source at a time to find the information needed to properly document it. Then have each person record the information in the format presented in the "Information" column.

Following this guided practice, have students use Simply Sources to record sources for a research project. After students conduct the research, show them how to use the organizer to prepare a formal bibliography. Provide a sample entry sheet so that students have a model to which they can refer.

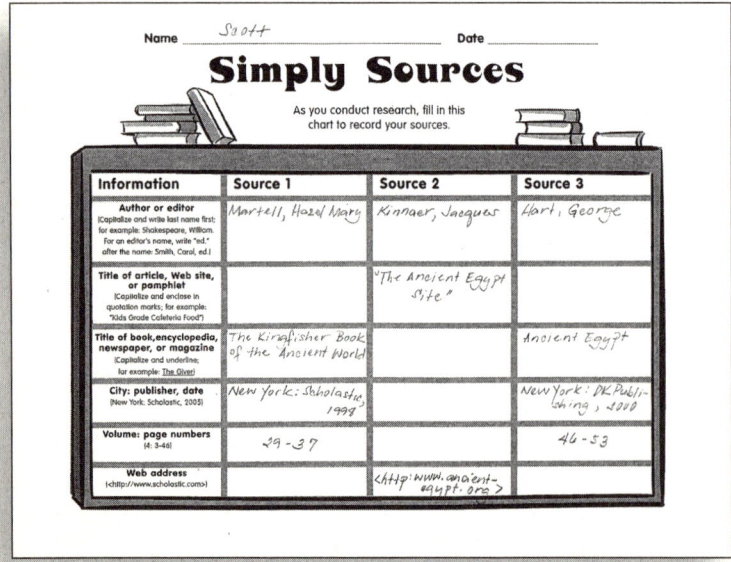

Name _____   Date _____

Simply Sources

As you conduct research, fill in this chart to record your sources.

Information	Source 1	Source 2	Source 3
Author or editor (Capitalize and write last name first; for example: Shakespeare, William. For an editor's name, write "ed." after the name: Smith, Carol, ed.)			
Title of article, Web site, or pamphlet (Capitalize and enclose in quotation marks; for example: "Kids Grade Cafeteria Food")			
Title of book, encyclopedia, newspaper, or magazine (Capitalize and underline; for example: The Giver)			
City: publisher, date (New York: Scholastic, 2005)			
Volume: page numbers (4: 3-46)			
Web address (<http://www.scholastic.com>)			

Bibliography

Bromley, K., L. Irwin-De Vitis, & M. Modlo. (1995). *Graphic Organizers: Visual Strategies for Active Learning.* New York: Scholastic Inc.

Boyle, J.R. & M. Weishaar. (1997). "The Effects of Expert-Generated Versus Student-Generated Cognitive Organizers on the Reading Comprehension of Students with Learning Disabilities." *Learning Disabilities Research and Practice*, 12(4), 228–235.

Chang, K.E., Y.T. Sung, & I.D. Chen. (2002). "The Effect of Concept Mapping to Enhance Text Comprehension and Summarization." *Journal of Experimental Education*, 71(1), 5–24.

Dodge, J. (2005). *Differentiation in Action.* New York: Scholastic Inc.

Ellis, E.S. (1994). "Integrating Writing Instruction with Content-Area Instruction: Part II: Writing Processes." *Intervention in School and Clinic*, 29(4), 219–230.

Guastello, E.F. (2000). "Concept Mapping Effects on Science Content Comprehension of Low-Achieving Inner-City Seventh Graders." *Remedial and Special Education*, 21(6), 356.

Moore, D. & J. Readence. (1984). "A Quantitative and Qualitative Review of Graphic Organizer Research." *Journal of Educational Research*, 78(1), 11–17.

National Center on Accessing the General Curriculum. (2002). http://www.cast.org/index.html